The Legacy of Billy Lee

An American Hero

Copyright © 2024 by Jon Andes

All rights reserved.

ISBN 978-1-62806-413-1 (print | paperback)
ISBN 978-1-62806-414-8 (print | hardback)
ISBN 978-1-62806-415-5 (ebook)

Library of Congress Control Number 2024916254

Published by Salt Water Media
29 Broad Street, Suite 104
Berlin, MD 21811
www.saltwatermedia.com

Illustrations by Olivia A. Momme

Portrait of George Washington and Billy Lee by John Trumbull
via metmuseum.org/art/collection/search/12822

Map of colonial Virginia from the Library of Congress
vialoc.gov/resource/g3880.ar139100/

The Legacy of Billy Lee

An American Hero

Written by Jon Andes

Illustrations by Olivia Momme

An Important Note

This is a story about the life and times of William "Billy" Lee. This is the story of an American hero. The story includes real dates and events in the life of Billy Lee. Information about enslaved people is missing from history. In some places, the author used his imagination to share details.

With Many Thanks

The publication of this book was made possible with the support of Salisbury University.

Dedication

This book is dedicated to the enslaved people who fought for our freedom.

Take a look at this painting.

Who do you see?

You may recognize George Washington,

who was the first president of the United States of America.

But who is the man in the background, holding the horse?

Why is this man in the painting?

What did he do?

This is the story of the man holding the horse.

William "Billy" Lee was filled with concern as he walked up the lane with his brother to their new home at the Mount Vernon plantation in the fall of 1767. He was a 16-year-old enslaved person. His thoughts swirled through his mind: *How would he be treated? What would the family be like? What would he do here? Where would he sleep? Would he make any friends? Would he ever be given his freedom?* He could not have imagined that he would become a witness to the birth of a nation, a personal aide to George Washington, and an American hero.

Billy was born in 1750 on Colonel Lee's plantation in the colony of Virginia. It was the custom at the time for enslaved people to take the last name of their plantation's owner. William, who went by Billy, was the property of the Lee family. As an enslaved person, he had no freedom. He could be bought and sold like any piece of property.

Billy was described as muscular and light-skinned or, in colonial language, a "Mulatto" man. He never knew his mother or father. All he knew was the rhythm of daily life on the Lee plantation.

Billy became an expert horseman while working as an enslaved person on the Lee plantation. One of his

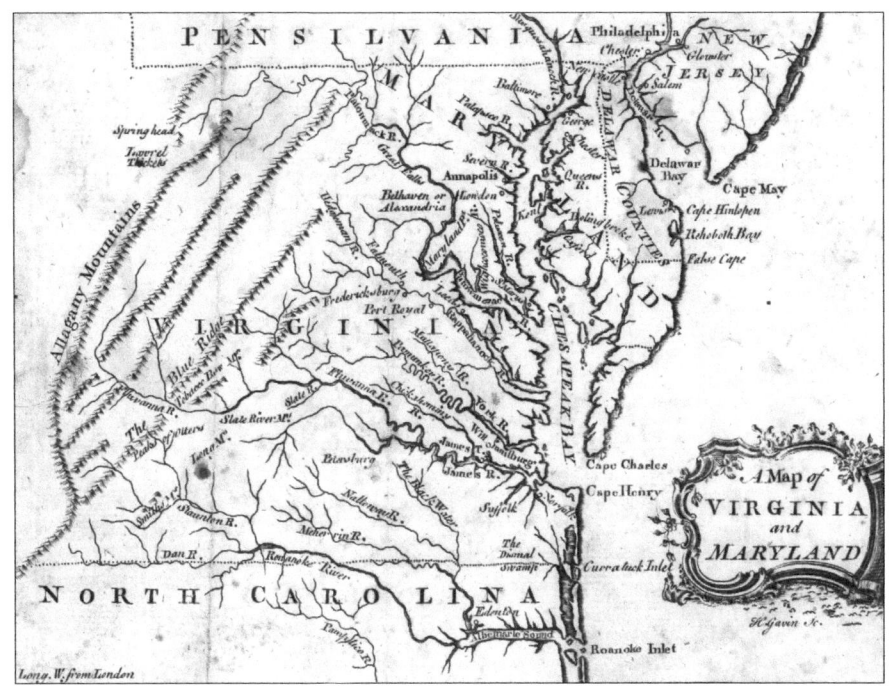

duties on the plantation was to accompany Colonel Lee and his guests on fox hunts. For plantation owners, fox hunting was a major social event lasting several days. Guests would be invited to participate in fox hunts and spend several days at a plantation. One of these hunts was where Billy first saw George Washington, who frequently attended Lee's fox hunts.

In the early spring of 1767, Colonel Lee died unexpectedly. As a result of his death, an estate sale was held at the plantation to sell Colonel Lee's property and slaves. Billy had to stand and watch the bidding as he was sold to George Washington for the price of 61 pounds and 15 shillings. This is about $10,000 in today's money. Filled with nerves and unanswered questions, Billy began the journey of several days that would end at his new home, George Washington's plantation, Mount Vernon.

At Mount Vernon, Billy quickly became known for his riding skills and his understanding of horses. He became the huntsman. This was a job with many responsibilities. As the huntsman, Billy took care of the horses and organized and prepared the riding horses for fox hunts. The duty of the huntsman was to ride out first to keep up with the hounds. Billy blew a hunting horn to alert the other riders of the direction of the fox. Billy rode a large, muscular chestnut horse named Cinkling. Billy and Cinkling would rush at full gallop across the field, fearlessly jumping hedgerows and ditches. Close behind Billy rode George Washington on Blueskin, a fiery, iron-gray horse. The success of the hunt depended on the skill of the huntsman.

The Mount Vernon plantation was over 8,000 acres, which is the equivalent of 12 ½ square miles. There were five outlying farms. Each farm had a farm manager, called an overseer, and a group of enslaved people. At the time, over 300 enslaved people lived on the plantation. Enslaved people who lived in wooden dirt floor cabins worked from first light to first dark six days per week. Every week on horseback, Washington, accompanied by Billy, would visit each of the outlying farms to check on the health of crops and the progress of clearing new farmland. Mount Vernon made Washington a very wealthy person.

Gradually, Billy became a much-entrusted member of the household. In addition to being the huntsman for Mount Vernon, Billy became Washington's manservant. As the manservant for Washington, Billy was responsible for taking care of Washington's clothing, footwear, and jewelry.

As well as looking after Washington's belongings, on many occasions, Billy traveled alone to deliver important documents and horses to other plantations. Because he was enslaved, Billy needed to have a travel permit or papers explaining his task when he traveled alone. Without one of these, he might be abducted by slave bounty hunters, lashed, and returned to the plantation or sold. Billy longed

to be free, but the escape to freedom was risky, and he could have been caught and sold.

Washington was a member of the Virginia colonial legislature. This was called the House of Burgesses, and Washington was a member for 15 years. Billy accompanied Washington when he traveled to Williamsburg, which was the capital of colonial Virginia. On these occasions, Billy's job was to take care of the horses and serve as a manservant to Washington. While in Williamsburg, Billy was in the company of the future leaders of the United States. Some of those leaders were Thomas Jefferson, George Mason, and Patrick Henry.

At this time, Virginia was a colony of England. Laws were passed by England's King and the British Parliament that demanded the purchase of certain items must include a tax. The money from these taxes was sent back to England. In the colonies, these laws became known as the "Intolerable Acts."

Representatives of each of the thirteen colonies met in Philadelphia in September of 1774. The gathering was called the First Continental Congress. Washington, as a member of the Virginia delegation to the Congress, traveled from Mount Vernon to Philadelphia. Once again, Billy accompanied Washington on the journey to serve as his manservant and take care of the horses.

On many occasions, Washington would entertain delegates at his Philadelphia home for dinner. Billy was often in the presence of people like Benjamin Franklin, John Adams, Patrick Henry, and Samuel Adams. With the adoption of a resolution condemning the "Intolerable Acts" by the Continental Congress, Washington and Billy returned to Mount Vernon.

Returning to fox hunts in Mount Vernon, visiting the five farms of the plantation, and preparing for winter occupied Billy. Life at Mount Vernon seemed to return to normal, but visitors often brought news of a rising conflict between the Colonies and England. More and more frequently, Washington held dinner parties with overnight guests.

Billy helped Washington organize and select clothing for each event, polished his boots and helped Washington get dressed. He was present at the dinner parties but, as an enslaved person, he was stationed quietly in the background, responding only when asked for assistance.

In the spring of 1775, the Second Continental Congress was held in Philadelphia. Washington, Billy, and other members of the household staff traveled to Philadelphia. On the brink of the war, which started in June of 1775, the Second Continental Congress chose Washington as the Commanding General of the Continental Army.

The army was assembled near Boston, a key port city. The British soldiers and Navy occupied Boston. To the cheers of many and the fears of others, Washington departed Philadelphia to assume command of the Continental Army. Billy accompanied Washington and proved to be an invaluable aide.

Upon arriving in Cambridge on the outskirts of Boston, Washington began the process of transforming a rag-tag group of 15,000 men into an army. In addition to his duties as a manservant, Billy was given the critically important task of storing and securing maps and Washington's highly valuable spyglass, otherwise known as a handheld telescope.

Each day, Billy would accompany Washington and other army officers on horseback to inspect the troops and climb a hill near Boston to watch for British troop movements. Washington used the spyglass to scan the city of Boston and to watch the movements of British ships and soldiers. The Continental Army had surrounded Boston, preventing supplies from reaching the British army by land.

For the Continental Army, the first winter in Cambridge was difficult. Supplies were short and the winter was cold. One day, when Washington and Billy were inspecting troops on horseback on Cambridge Commons, a brawl broke out among the soldiers. Nearly, 1,000 soldiers were punching and kicking each other. Washington spurred his horse and raced into the soldiers with Billy following close behind.

Washington dismounted and began stepping between soldiers to stop the fighting. Billy grabbed the reins of Washington's horse and held him steady and moved into the crowd to help Washington. With Billy on horseback pushing the crowd back and Washington on foot, the brawl stopped, and order was restored.

For nearly one year, Washington and the Continental Army laid siege to Boston. On March 17, 1776,

Washington and Billy rode to the heights overlooking Boston along with other Continental Army officers.

Looking toward the port as he handed the spyglass to Washington, Billy could barely see British ships sailing out of the port of Boston. Using the spyglass, Washington confirmed that British soldiers, sailors, and ships were leaving Boston. Washington and the army officers began to speculate about the possible destination of the British fleet, sailors, and soldiers.

From reliable spies and other sources, Washington learned that the British fleet was traveling from Boston to New York. Washington knew that the port of New York would be critical to the success of the Continental Army. With the withdrawal of the British from Boston, Washington gave orders for the Continental Army to march to New York to defend the city and win the war. For this journey, Billy was entrusted with carrying the critically important maps, papers, and correspondence, as well as the spyglass. The highly valuable papers included the battle plans for the Continental Army.

Reaching New York City, Washington found the British fleet had arrived and British soldiers were landing to occupy New York. Billy attended an officers' meeting that included Alexander Hamilton and Lafayette. At this meeting, the strategy for the battle was finalized. To prevent the British from taking New York, the Continental Army would attack the British on Long Island.

With Billy at his side, Washington directed the attack from a distance. As the battle began, Washington could see from his spyglass that the Continental Army was losing. As Washington rode forward to rally the troops, Billy charged into battle. The troops were quickly overwhelmed. For fear of Washington being captured or wounded, Billy encouraged him to withdraw from the battle. With the battle for New York City lost, Washington ordered a retreat across the Hudson River at night into the safe area of New Jersey.

The battle of New York was a disaster for the Continental Army. On horseback, in the light of the sunrise, Washington and Billy looked over the cliffs of the palisades on the east side of the Hudson River. They watched as the remaining soldiers crossed the river from New York to New Jersey. Washington asked Billy for his spyglass so that he could try to count the number of boats and escaping soldiers. As Washington contemplated finding a safe place for the soldiers to rest, Billy handed Washington the precious maps to plot a course to safety.

After consulting with fellow officers, Washington decided to seek refuge for the Continental Army in Pennsylvania at Valley Forge, near Philadelphia. The Continental Army marched through New Jersey into Pennsylvania. A camp and buildings were erected at Valley Forge. At this camp, Billy continued to attend to Washington's needs as his manservant. When Washington rode on horseback to inspect the troops, Billy rode with him. As Washington met with commanding officers to plot the army's next move, Billy went with him, providing the critical maps and papers.

The British had taken Philadelphia. Valley Forge was 25 miles west of Philadelphia. Washington knew that he could not attack Philadelphia. A British garrison at Princeton, New Jersey would be a possible target. However, to attack Princeton in winter, the army would need to cross the ice-packed Delaware River.

To take advantage of the element of surprise, Washington ordered an attack on Christmas Eve of 1776. With Billy at his side, Washington and the Continental Army crossed the Delaware River, surprising the garrison at Princeton and winning an important victory.

With the British still occupying Philadelphia after the victory at Princeton, Washington and the army retreated to the safety of Valley Forge. The winter was very cold, and supplies were limited. The conditions for the soldiers were severe. Rising at first light, Billy continued to take care of Washington's daily needs. Each day, with his fellow officers and Billy at his side, Washington would visit the troops and try to sustain their well-being.

The country of France entered the war to help the Colonies. The British troops in Philadelphia were ordered to travel to New York to defend New York City from a possible blockade by the French fleet or an invasion by the French army. With word that the British were leaving Philadelphia, Billy accompanied Washington as he met with his officers to plan an attack. Washington and the other officers decided to intercept and attack the British army as the troops moved through New Jersey.

As the Continental Army marched from Valley Forge, Pennsylvania toward the British army, the summer weather turned very hot. After several

days of marching, the Continental Army engaged the British army at Monmouth, New Jersey. With Billy at his side on horseback, Washington used his spyglass to observe the fighting. As the battle continued, the Continental Army seemed to be losing.

To save the day for the Continental Army, Washington and Billy raced at full gallop into the battle to rally the troops. In the heat of battle and with bullets flying all around them, Washington's horse collapsed. Seeing the danger for Washington, Billy charged forward. With bullets and cannon fire blazing from all sides, Billy brought a spare horse to Washington. Once again, Billy saved Washington from capture or death. Exhausted and battle weary, the Continental Army camped in New Jersey.

News came to Washington's headquarters that the French fleet had driven the British ships from the Chesapeake Bay. The British army in Virginia was trapped at the port town of Yorktown. Washington, Billy, and several divisions of the Continental Army quickly traveled south from Pennsylvania to Virginia.

Upon arrival at Yorktown, Virginia, battle plans were put in place to lay siege. With no escape available, the British troops were surrounded. On October 19, 1781, the British army surrendered. As the British soldiers marched from Yorktown in defeat, Washington, Continental Army officers, and Billy watched the proceedings on horseback. The colonies had won the War for Independence. Washington was the war hero who secured independence for the colonies and Billy was the enslaved manservant, groom, and aide to Washington who helped to make the colonies free.

Once the British army had withdrawn from New York, Washington and Billy began the journey home to Mount Vernon, reaching Annapolis, Maryland on December 23, 1783. At the Maryland State Capital building, Billy looked on as General Washington resigned from his post as Commander of the Continental Army. A grateful nation thanked Washington for his service to the new country.

Washington and Billy had spent eight years at war, traveling thousands of miles together on horseback. They encountered all types of weather and fought a war to win freedom for a new nation. Through triumph and loss, Billy was always present with Washington. With the end of the war, Washington and Billy traveled back to Mount Vernon, where

Washington was a hero and Billy was an enslaved person. In four short years, Washington and Billy would be called back to serve their new country.

Washington was happy to be back at Mount Vernon. He wanted to live out the rest of his life as a plantation owner and farmer. Billy resumed his duties as huntsman and groom, taking care of Washington's personal needs. The eight years of war had taken a physical toll on both Washington and Billy. Both men were older and suffered from physical ailments. One day, on a surveying trip with Washington to settle a boundary dispute, Billy suffered a very serious knee injury. The injury made it very difficult for Billy to walk and ride.

With the independence and freedom that Billy and Washington helped to win for the new nation—the United States of America—it became apparent that a new type of government was needed. In the spring of 1787, once again, Washington and Billy traveled to Philadelphia, Pennsylvania to attend a constitutional convention. The meetings were held at Independence Hall.

Washington and Billy spent four hot summer months in Philadelphia. Delegates arrived from all the former colonies. Washington was elected to preside over the meetings of the delegates. During this time, Billy continued to act as an enslaved manservant to Washington, taking care of his clothing, personal needs, and correspondence with other delegates.

On numerous occasions, Washington and Billy would walk the streets of Philadelphia at first light. People who admired Washington would stop to speak with him. By this time, Pennsylvania had made slavery illegal. Billy was an enslaved person living in a place where slavery was illegal. Debates at the Continental Congress included an intense and heated argument over the future of slavery.

During the Revolutionary War, approximately 5,000 enslaved people were soldiers in the Continental Army, fighting to create a nation free from colonial rule. Northern states wanted to abolish slavery, and southern states demanded that slavery continue. At the Continental Congress, a compromise was reached to allow slavery to continue. For the purposes of determining the number of representatives from each state in the new Congress, enslaved people would only count at three-fifths of a person.

With the ratification of the new Constitution by the states, Washington was unanimously elected President of the United States of America. New York City was selected as the capital of the new nation. A three-story mansion became the new home of the president. In New York City, on April 30, 1789, Washington became the first President of the United States, and Billy became the enslaved manservant and valet to the new President.

Service in the war had taken a physical toll on Billy. Lack of sleep, improper nutrition, and riding thousands of miles on horseback proved to be too much for his legs. Billy found it very difficult to climb the steps of the presidential mansion in New York City. The pain in his legs was too much to tolerate. It was decided that Billy would return to Mount Vernon.

As Billy recuperated at Mount Vernon, he became an expert at leatherwork, repairing boots, saddles, bridles, harnesses, and other types of leather goods. In the spring of 1797, after serving as President for two terms, a total of eight years, Washington retired to Mount Vernon.

At Mount Vernon, Washington resumed his duties as a plantation owner and farmer. The war and the presidential duties had taken a toll on Washington as well. Failing health and physical ailments plagued him.

Nearly two years after returning home to Mount Vernon, with friends and family at his bed and Billy in the room, Washington died on December 14, 1799. He was buried in a tomb at Mount Vernon. From the fields of Mount Vernon to the fields of war and later to the presidential mansion, Billy had served Washington for over thirty years, taking care of Washington's every need and, on at least two occasions, saving his life.

Several days after Washington's funeral, with the family gathered in the main room of Mount Vernon and Billy in the kitchen, Washington's will was read to the family by a lawyer. As Billy listened through the kitchen door, he heard the simple but life-changing words, for "...his faithful services during the Revolutionary War...," Billy Lee was now free. He would receive an allowance and be able to live at Mount Vernon. Hearing that he was free, Billy walked out the back door of the house and gazed at the horizon. He was finally a freeman, but he was the only slave granted freedom by Washington. Over three hundred other African American people remained enslaved at Mount Vernon.

As a freeman, Billy decided to stay at Mount Vernon. Over the years, former Continental Army officers and soldiers would travel to Mount Vernon to visit the grave of Washington and chat with Billy. In 1827, the Marquis de Lafayette of France, an officer and hero who brilliantly served with Washington, traveled from France to visit Mount Vernon for the last time. Billy and Lafayette spent many hours talking about the years spent together in battle. They reminisced about Washington, their miles spent riding together, the cold of Valley Forge, the Christmas Eve surprise attack on Trenton, and the surrender of the British army at Yorktown. It would be one of the last times that Billy would meet with a former army officer.

In 1828, Billy died at the age of 77. He is buried in an unmarked grave in the cemetery for enslaved people at Mount Vernon. In a society that enslaved him, Billy gave his talents and labor and risked his life for the cause of freedom for others. Without his service, the United States may not have become a free nation. William "Billy" Lee, born an enslaved person and yearning for freedom, was and will always be an American hero.

And to my Mulatto man William calling himself Billy Lee, I give immediate freedom ...for his faithful services during the Revolutionary War.

References

Davis, K. C. (2016). *In the shadow of liberty: The hidden history of slavery, four presidents, and five Black lives.* Henry Holt and Company.

Lamensdorf, L. (2012). *The ballad of Billy Lee.* Seascape Press.

Thompson, J. C. (2015). *George Washington's mulatto man.* Commonwealth Book Publishers of Virginia.

William "Billy" Lee, The National Library for the Study of George Washington at Mount Vernon, retrieved from https://www.mountvernon.org/library/digitalhistory/digital-encyclopedia/article/william-billy-lee/

Major Events in the Life of William Billy Lee:

Early Life:

- Born 1750 as an Enslaved Person
- Lives on the Plantation of Colonel John Lee, Cabin Point, Virginia
- Becomes an Expert Rider and Horseman
- Sold to George Washington April 1767

Life at Mount Vernon:

- Arrives at Mount Vernon Plantation October 1767
- Becomes Huntsman Responsible for Horses and Organizing the Fox Hunt
- Exploration to Blue Ridge Mountains September 1770
- Becomes Valet or Manservant to Washington
- Travels with Washington to Virginia House of Burgesses in Williamsburg, Virginia

Commander in Chief:

- Travels with Washington to the First Continental Congress Philadelphia September 1774

- Washington Selected as Commander and Chief of the Continental Army 16 June 1775
- Travels with Washington to Boston to Command the Continental Army 1 July 1775
- Helps Washington Quell Brawl of Soldiers in Cambridge March 1776
- British Army Leaves Bost and Sails to New York March 1776
- Washington and Billy Arrive in New York April 1776
- Declaration of Independence Signed 4 July 1776
- Continental Army Evacuates Long Island August 1776
- Continental Army Suffers Defeat in New York September 1776
- Continental Army Escapes from New York October 1776
- Continental Army Travels Across New Jersey to the Safety of Valley Forge, Pennsylvania November 1776
- Continental Army Attacks and Captures Trenton and Princeton, New Jersey 26 December 1776
- Continental Army Camps at Morristown, New Jersey January – June 1777
- British Army Moves to Capture Philadelphia, Pennsylvania with Multiple Battles August – October 1777
- Continental Army Retreats to Valley Forge, Pennsylvania November – March 1778
- Continental Army Attacks British at Monmouth, New Jersey June 1778
- French Forces Join the Continental Army August 1778
- Continental Army Camps near New York City to Observe British in New York Winter 1778 – 1779
- Continental Army Remains in New York Area to Deter British Attack 1780 - 81
- British Army Under the Command of Cornwallis Arrive at Yorktown, Virginia August 1781
- Continental Army Moves from New York to Virginia to Attack the British Army
- French Fleet Defeat the British Fleet September 1781
- Continental Army and French Forces Surround British Army at Yorktown, Virginia
- British Army Surrenders to Washington 19 October 1781
- Washington and Billy Lee Return to Mount Vernon November 1781
- Washington and Billy Lee Travel to New York to Oversee the Withdrawal of British Forces From New York March 1782 – November 1783

- Washington Bids Farewell to Officers in New York December 1783
- Washington Resigns as Commander in Chief of the Continental Army 23 December 1783
- Washington and Billy Return to Mount Vernon to a Hero's Welcome December 1783
- Surveying with Washington Billy Breaks Kneecap April 1785

Serving the President:

- Washington and Billy travel to Philadelphia for the Constitutional Convention May 1787
- United States Constitution Adopted September 1787
- United States Constitution Ratified July 1788
- Washington Elected First President of the United States January 1789
- Washington Travels to New York to Serve as President April 1789
- Serves as Butler to President Washington
- Washington Retires as President March 1797

Return to Mount Vernon:

- Washington Oversees Plantation with Billy
- Washington Dies 14 December 1799 and Buried at Mount Vernon
- Washington Will Sets Billy Free and Provides a Monthly Allowance

Life After Washington:

- Billy Lives at Mount Vernon Serving as a Cobbler and Leather Worker
- Former Revolutionary War Officers Visit the Grave of Washington at Mount Vernon and Share Stories with Billy
- Lafayette Visits Mount Vernon and Shares Stories with Billy
- Billy Dies in 1828 and Buried in the Slave Cemetery in an Unmarked Grave at Mount Vernon

About the Author: Jon Andes

Jon Andes, Ed.D. has been involved in public education for nearly 50 years. He began his teaching career as a social studies teacher at Havre De Grace High School. In addition to teaching, he has been a high school coach, assistant principal, principal, assistant superintendent, superintendent of schools, and a board of education member. He currently teaches in the Department of Leadership and Literacy Studies at Salisbury University.

About the Illustrator: Olivia Momme

Olivia's parents told her she could be anything she wanted, so she became an artist. She received her Bachelors of Fine Arts degree with a concentration in photography from Salisbury University. While her chosen mediums are usually photography and painting, she was inspired by her college drawing professor, Ed Brown, to pursue illustration. She continues to follow her passion for art while being the Director of the Worcester County Education Foundation on the Eastern Shore of Maryland.

www.ingramcontent.com/pod-product-compliance
Lightning Source LLC
LaVergne TN
LVHW070909080426
835510LV00005B/125